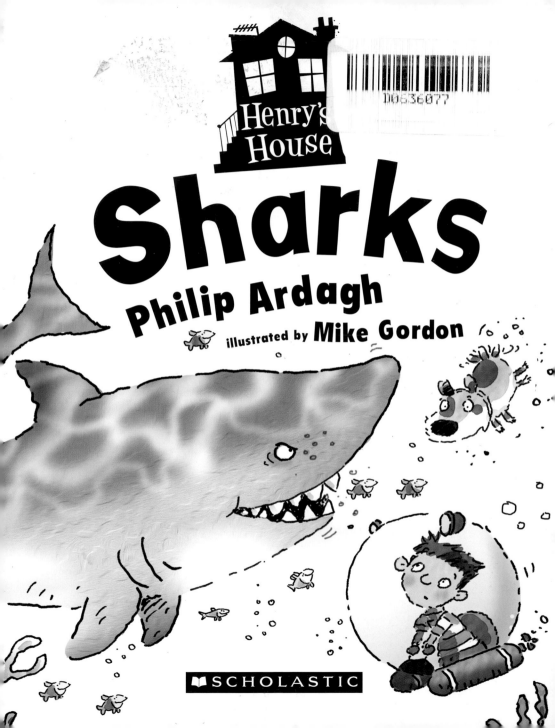

Henry's House

Sharks

Philip Ardagh

illustrated by **Mike Gordon**

SCHOLASTIC

For Freddie and the minnows.

P.A.

Senior Editor: Jill Sawyer

Scholastic Children's Books,
Euston House, 24 Eversholt Street,
London NW1 1DB, UK
a division of Scholastic Ltd
London ~ New York ~ Toronto ~ Sydney ~ Auckland
Mexico City ~ New Delhi ~ Hong Kong

First published in the UK by Scholastic Ltd, 2013

ISBN 978 1407 11485 9

Printed and bound by Tien Wah Press Pte. Ltd, Singapore

10 9 8 7 6 5 4 3 2 1

Philip Ardagh and **Mike Gordon** are regular visitors to Henry's House. Philip (the one with the beard) keeps a note of everything that's going on, and even reads a mind or two. Mike (the one without the beard) sketches whatever he sees, however fantastical it may be ... and together they bring you the adventures of Henry, an ordinary boy in an extraordinary house!

Contents

Welcome to Henry's House!

Taking a shower

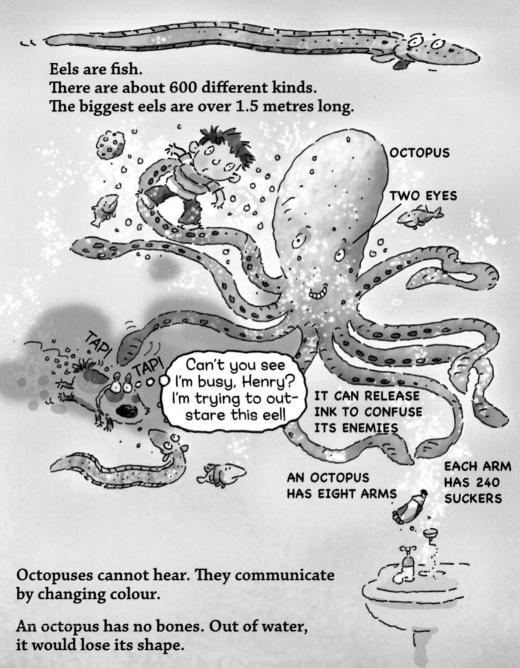

Eels are fish.
There are about 600 different kinds.
The biggest eels are over 1.5 metres long.

Octopuses cannot hear. They communicate
by changing colour.

An octopus has no bones. Out of water,
it would lose its shape.

Through the porthole

The average depth of the seas and oceans is 2.4 miles (3.8 km).

Scientists divide seas and oceans into three zones:
THE SUNLIT ZONE (from the surface to 200 metres) contains the most wildlife.

THE TWILIGHT ZONE (from 200 metres to 1,000 metres).

THE DARK ZONE (below 1,000 metres) is pitch black and lived in by creepy-looking animals. Some even glow in the dark!

A drop in the ocean

10

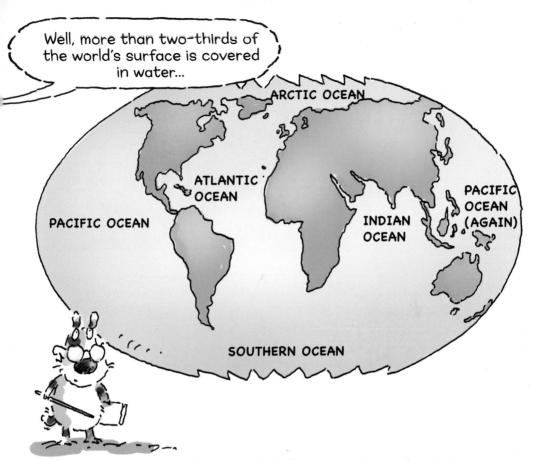

On a round globe, that bit of the Pacific joins up with the other bit over there, to make one BIG ocean.

Ninety-seven per cent of water on Earth is (salty) sea water.

Winds make waves that make currents on the surface of the sea.

The pull of the Moon creates tides, seen as the going-out and coming-in of the sea on beaches.

Feeling crabby

There are just under 6,800 different types of crab around the world.

Some spend all of their time underwater. Some spend some time on land.

Crabs are crustaceans.

Most crabs have one front claw bigger than the other.

Crabs walk 'sideways'.

Crabs can live up to 60 years.

The biggest crab is the giant spider crab. Its claw span can be up to 4 metres.

FLAT BODY

SHELL

TEN LEGS

Smellies and jellies

Whale of a time

* Whales are mammals, not fish. They are warm-blooded, and their babies drink milk.

BLOW HOLE

TAIL

*They have to come to the surface to breathe in fresh air. They breathe through their blow holes, blowing stale air and water vapour up into the air before breathing in fresh air.

NOTCH

FLUKES

THICK LAYER OF BLUBBER

*Their tails stick out sideways (horizontally) rather than upwards and downwards (vertically) like fish tails.

*Whales can be so HUGE because the seawater supports their weight.

Narwhals and killer whales are toothed whales.

Humpback whales are one of a group of whales, called baleen whales, which includes blue whales.

Humpback whales don't have teeth.

18

There are over seventy species of whale. Some, like this orca, swim in groups, called pods.

Orcas can travel faster than a speedboat.

Aha! Sweeeeet. Hello, Orca!

BLUE WHALE
BIGGEST WHALE
AND BIGGEST ANIMAL
ON EARTH OVER
30.5 METRES LONG

FIN WHALE
26.8 METRES LONG

SPERM WHALE
18 METRES LONG

HUMPBACK WHALE
15.2 METRES LONG

MOTHBALL
SMALL DOG

20

Whaling

- People have been hunting whales for over 5,000 years. This is called whaling.

- Whales were hunted for meat, fat, oil, leather and bone.

- There were huge fleets of whaling ships in the eighteenth and nineteenth centuries.

- Even in the 1930s more than 50,000 whales were killed a year.

- In 1986 whaling was banned.

- Some countries still kill whales which they claim are not endangered.

- Charities such as Greenpeace argue that no whales should be killed.

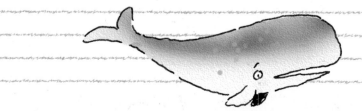

22

23

Why do dolphins also make that weird clicking noise?

It's a kind of underwater radar. Look...

- The clicks bounce back off whatever's in the water in front of the dolphin.

- The bounced-back clicks return to the dolphin where they're turned into a sound map in their brain. This creates a 'mental picture' of what's out there.

- As well as being a good way to find food, they can also use it to avoid enemies and obstacles.

Dolphins are very smart creatures.

Smart? Ha! I bet they don't know what the capital of Brazil is.

25

26

Sharks' skeletons are made of cartilage, making them very flexible.

What do you mean "touch my toes"? I don't have any toes.

• Sharks have the most powerful jaws of any animal.
• They have 'back-up' teeth. If a tooth breaks another one swivels into place.
• A shark can grow up to 20,000 teeth in its lifetime.

That saves on dentists' bills!

Sharks usually eat alone. If there's more than one shark, they often end up biting each other!

Table for one, sir?

Freeze!

It's not following us... It's too busy eating Mothball's meal.

The cheek of it!

MUNCH!

MUNCH!

PANT! PANT!

POLAR BEARS:

Are the world's biggest bears.

Are the biggest meat-eater on land (even if that 'land' is really ice).

Spend most of their lives on the sea, floating on chunks of ice (called ice floes).

Are excellent swimmers. They can swim up to 25 miles/40 km in one go.

Are furry on the outside with a layer of blubber under the skin protect them from the freezing cold.

Deal with seals

35

Sneaky beakies

Some people think penguins look 'funny' as they waddle on land.

Underwater, they are amazing swimmers.

Three layers of overlapping feathers keep them warm and waterproof.

Penguins can't fly. They use their flippers like oars.

Penguins' big webbed feet make excellent rudders for steering through the sea.

EMPEROR PENGUIN

On land, they huddle together in large groups to keep warm.

Emperor penguins are the biggest penguins.

Freezing winds travel at more than 100 mph/ 160 kmph.

HENRY'S HANDY PENGUIN GUIDE

• There are 17 or 18 different types of penguin. Experts can't agree!
• Not ALL penguins live in the Antarctic. For example, African penguins live off the southern coast of Africa.

Types of penguin include:

1 Emperor penguins: the dad looks after the egg while the mum goes hunting for fish for months.

2 Chinstrap penguins: sometimes called bearded penguins – are small but fierce. They'll chase away bigger penguins that get too close to their nests.

3 King penguins: look slimmer and more upright (more 'human') than other penguins.

4 Humboldt penguins: have black faces and a horseshoe-shaped marking on their chests. They live off the coast of South America.

5 Rockhopper penguins: have colourful head feathers or 'crests'. They get their name from hopping from rock to rock!

1　　2　　3　　4　　5

Reef!

Huh? What? I must have drifted off to sleep...

ZZZZZ!

WORMS

FISH

SEA SQUIRTS

MOLLUSCS

SEA ANEMONES

Coral are tiny sea creatures.

They ooze something called calcium carbonate.

This hardens to create a coral reef.

Coral reefs are home to all sorts of undersea life.

There are three main types of reef:

1 Fringing reef – attached to the shore or right by it.

2 Barrier reef – separated from the shore by a deep channel or a lagoon.

3 Atoll reef – barrier reef which forms (or almost forms) a circle.

Clownfish poo is good for anemones too!

CLOWNFISH

Go on. Make me laugh. I dare you.

Clownfish are also called anemonefish because they have a special relationship with sea anemones.

Anemones have a poisonous sting which they use to kill other animals.

They don't harm clownfish. Clownfish eat the little creatures which could harm them.

WORKING TOGETHER

Anemones have a special relationship with hermit crabs.

When the hermit crab finds an old shell to live in, an anemone often moves onto it.

When the crab grows and moves into a bigger shell, the anemone moves with it.

The anemone protects the hermit crab and the crab acts as the anemone's 'driver', increasing its chances of finding food!

FISHY FRIENDS

Some fish are friendlier than others. They not only get on well in their own group but with other types of fish.

A different kind of bed

It's amazing what you find on the seabed.

You can hardly see these fish. They're really flat and the colour of sand.

Some can change colour to match different backgrounds.

SOLE

PLAICE

Look a starfish!

The correct name for them is actually 'sea stars'. Although many species have five legs, some have MANY more. If they lose a leg, a new one will grow.

Wow! Imagine a bowl of dog food that always grew back.

This is an oyster, where natural pearls come from. Natural pearls are very rare.

THE OYSTER AND THE PEARL

PEARL NECKLACE

A piece of shell or grit gets into the oyster's shell. To stop it irritating, the oyster coats it in a special coating, layer by layer. Over time, this forms a pearl.

Cultured pearls are like real pearls except humans put the tiny piece of shell in oysters in the first place. They are still 'real' pearls, but cost much less.

What are you? Underwater hedgehogs?

'Urchin' is an old name for 'hedgehog'.

SEA URCHIN

Look, here are some sand dollars. You can sometimes find their skeletons on the beach.

Whoa! Why's it gone dark?

Soaking up some rays

47

Undercover underwater

UNDERSEA DISGUISE ARTISTS

* Stonefish look like stone.

* Angel fish look like plants or coral.

*The mimic octopus disguises itself as dangerous animals, such as a lion fish, a poisonous sole or even as lots of poisonous sea snakes!

* This leafy sea dragon really does look like LEAVES!

* Cuttlefish can change colour at very high speed to fit in with their changing surroundings.

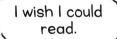

I wish I could read.

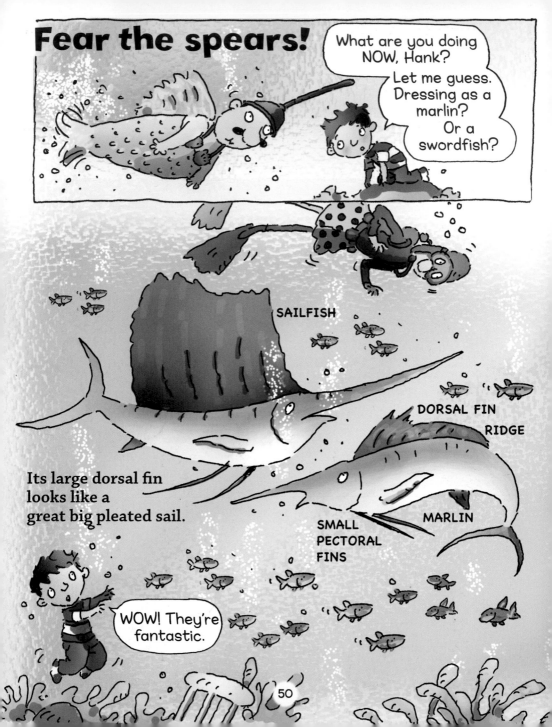

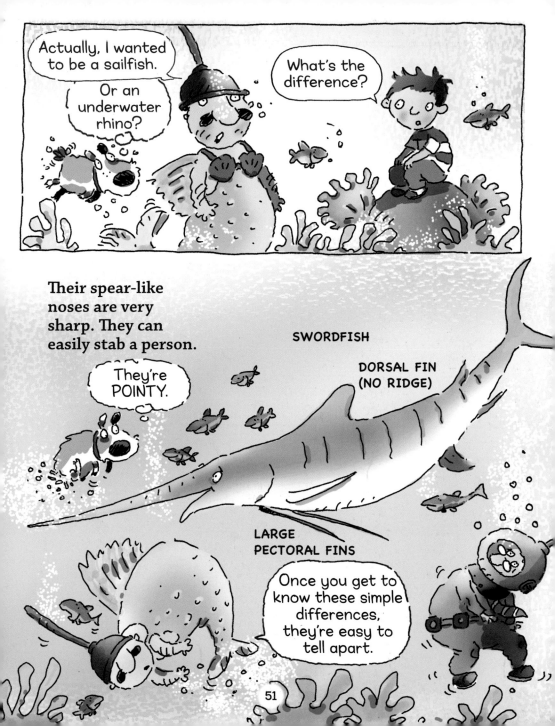

Actually, I wanted to be a sailfish.

Or an underwater rhino?

What's the difference?

Their spear-like noses are very sharp. They can easily stab a person.

They're POINTY.

SWORDFISH

DORSAL FIN (NO RIDGE)

LARGE PECTORAL FINS

Once you get to know these simple differences, they're easy to tell apart.

Danger! Danger!

If puffer fish are about to be attacked, they swallow water and 'puff out' to make themselves much bigger.

If swallowed, they release the toxin which is horrible-tasting to most predators.

To humans, the pufferfish's poison is 1,200 times more deadly than cyanide.

Not all types of pufferfish have spikes.

Highs and lows

- An albatross can have a wingspan of up to 3.6 metres.
- They can glide for hours without flapping their wings even once.
- They can live up to 50 years, spending most of their time away from land.
- Some sailors thought it bad luck to kill an albatross.

55

On solid ground

Henry's room. One hour later...

That was amazing! Wasn't it great to get up close to all those sea creatures, Mothball?

The ones who didn't want to eat my food ... or US.

But it's good to have things back to normal.

NORMAL, Henry? You do know that thing you're leaning against is a giant turtle...?

And that's not another DOG barking out in the garden...

...but a SEA LION!

Sea lions bark. Seals don't. Sea lions have big flippers and can walk on all fours. Seals can't.

SEA LION

ARF!

ARF!

WALRUS

HUGE TUSKS

And look at that sandpit!

Turtles lay their eggs in the sand.

When the babies hatch they have to find their way down to the sea.

Very few make it to adulthood. (Turtles can live to over 100.)

Once in the sea, a male turtle is unlikely to set foot on land again. (A female may return to lay eggs of her own.)

Come away from the window, Mothball. Time for a snooze. And who knows what our NEXT adventure will be...

WAG!
WAG!
WAG!

Shark Chart

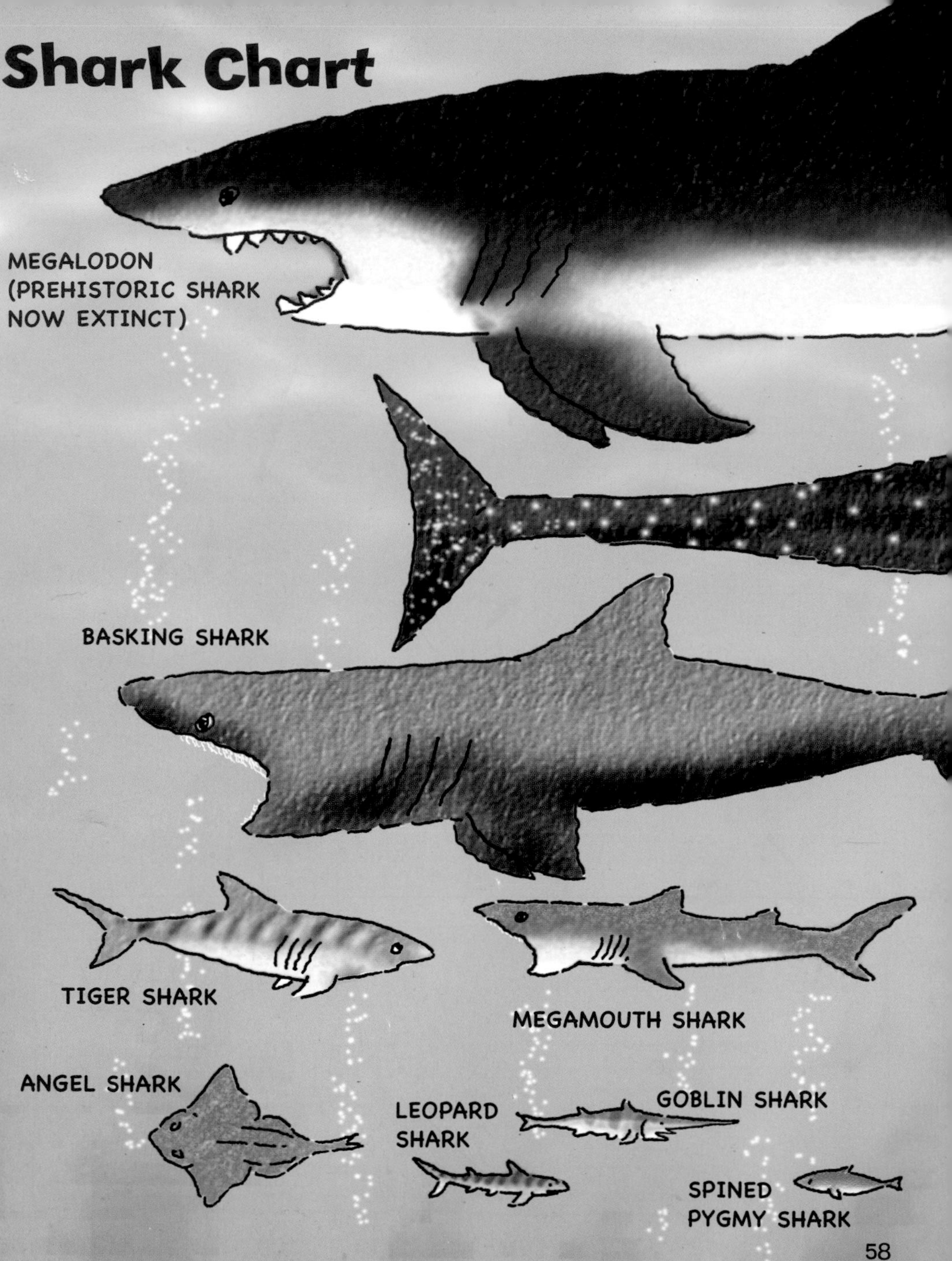

MEGALODON
(PREHISTORIC SHARK
NOW EXTINCT)

BASKING SHARK

TIGER SHARK

MEGAMOUTH SHARK

ANGEL SHARK

LEOPARD
SHARK

GOBLIN SHARK

SPINED
PYGMY SHARK

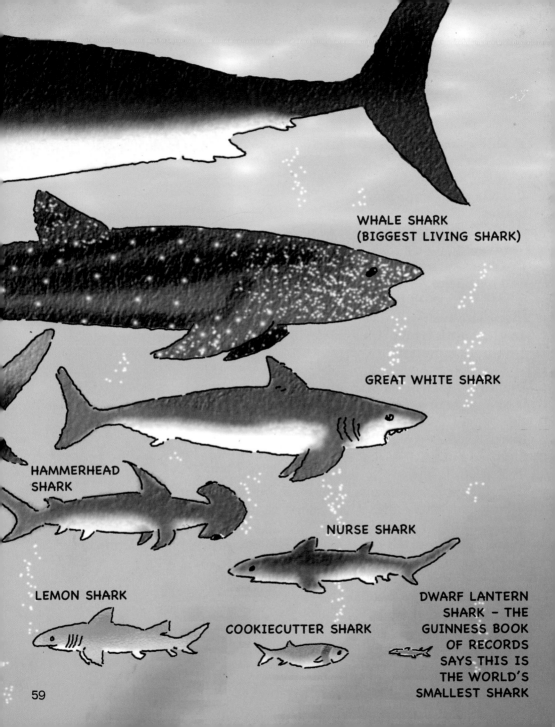

WHALE SHARK
(BIGGEST LIVING SHARK)

GREAT WHITE SHARK

HAMMERHEAD
SHARK

NURSE SHARK

LEMON SHARK

COOKIECUTTER SHARK

DWARF LANTERN
SHARK – THE
GUINNESS BOOK
OF RECORDS
SAYS THIS IS
THE WORLD'S
SMALLEST SHARK

Glossary

Angler fish: a deep-sea fish that gets its name from its fin which looks like a fishing rod.

Blubber: a layer of oil and fat under the skin which keeps sea mammals, such as whales and seals, warm.

Cartilage: a bendy material – a bit like bone – found in many animals' bodies – including humans. Some fishes, such as skates and rays, have whole skeletons made of cartilage.

Crustacean: a big family of animals that includes crabs, lobsters, krill and barnacles.

Elephant seal: called this because the male seal's snout looks a bit like an elephant's trunk. They can hold their breath underwater for up to 1 hour 40 minutes.

Endangered: when a plant or animal species is in danger of dying out – becoming extinct.

Extinct: when a plant or animal species has died out.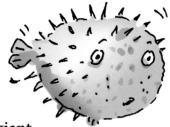

Giant isopod: a deep-sea creature a bit like a giant woodlouse. It rolls into a ball at any sign of trouble.

Giant squid: related to octopuses, it's the world's biggest animal without a backbone.

Gulper eel: a deep-sea fish. Its large, loose jaw means it can catch food far bigger than it is!

Ink: a dark-coloured liquid which octopuses and squid are able to squirt into water to hide themselves from attackers.

Krill: tiny shrimplike creatures that many types of whale like to eat.

Lobsters: ten-legged crustaceans: are closely related to crabs, shrimp and krill.

Long-nosed chimaera: a deep-sea fish. Sometimes called a 'ghost shark'. Its poisonous tail could kill a person.

Mollusc: a huge family of animals without backbones. There are over 85,000 different types of mollusc. Octopuses and squids are molluscs. Oysters are too.

Octopus: a member of the mollusc family. Biggest octopus: Giant Pacific (up to 9 metres). Smallest: Californian octopus (as small as 1 cm).

Radar: an object-detection system that uses radio waves. Dolphins use a similar system that allows them to detect creatures in the water.

Sand dollar: a flat round type of sea urchin. It's called this because it looks a bit like a coin. (And there's an American coin called a dollar.)

Sea sponge: not a plant, not a coral, but an animal (even though it has no brain).

Starship Enterprise: a spaceship that appears in *Star Trek* the TV series, books and films. It looks a bit like a giant ray.

Suckers: areas on octopuses' and squids' arms and tentacles, a bit like tiny mouths, which catch on and hold on to their prey.

Wingspan: the distance measured from one bird's wing-tip to the other when their wings are spread out.

Index

Henry's House

We hope you enjoyed your visit

to Henry's House

Come back soon!

Look out for: • Bodies • Dinosaurs • Space
• Creepy-crawlies • Egyptians • Romans
• Knights and Castles

For more facts and fun, visit us at
www.headforhenryshouse.co.uk